With love

#Oh_My_George

# WHEN THERE'S TOO MUCH ON

# TOP

# JUST STOP

The fine line

between

**INSANITY**

**GENIUS**

**&**

**MENTAL HEALTH**

Are we Conscious?

George Boyle

@GCMind

# Contents

# Acknowledgements

I will like to say a huge thank you to the universe for guiding me to write this book in these moments in times of awakening around our abilities as human beings and our thoughts around mental health

Thank you for the inspiration by the whole of the team at schoolofawakening and akashic guys, Andy Harrington, David Shepherd, Bev James and more.

Many parts of this book have been created from the learnings I have been blessed to acknowledge and help me overcome my sound of what mental health was too myself to empower and encourage me always, to be part of an amazing world supportive community.

I will like to thank some social media sights for all inspiration, any thoughts captured or obtained within my own research into the thoughts or reactions from many who I may have encountered whilst writing this and hope that now will appreciate you have read this short book, and hope it may make a difference to how you create your own thoughts to creating a relationship.

I will like to thank personally Surina, I love you so much for the inspiration for the title of this book. Yvette for Our Monkey Minds, Bevell for his magical poetry and words. Rhaveen and Catherine for making sure I got on board at the right time.

I thank society for being such a fuck up to make me so passionate to make a difference to mental health, and to get people to wake up and stop treating each other like shit within the learnings and writings within this book

I love and thank my parents, my family and forgive them for not understanding at times

I thank my daft old rescue dog Tess bless her if she will make it through who is near on 18. and my cats past and present Sox.

I will love to thank all the amazing people in the background that have helped support me when others have failed to do so, those who have recognition and have been a beam of light and support.

I will love to thank the Rhoud Singh Family for all there understandings and support, and my friend David Jones for being there in the last 10yrs, and Anna.

To Sidra Jafri for writing a book to bring an Awakening to people worldwide.

# Foreword

You may be wondering why choose this subject?

## Mental Health.

The truth be it, is that everyone has a form of mental health, It's just that we all manage it in different ways.

Or that that form becomes a pressure where our physical emotional and spiritual health is imbalanced, so that we are not in a state of flow or mind to manage or cope with our mental health which causes problems and issues with our Spiritual, Physical and emotional.

Einstein once quoted that there is a fine line between genius and insanity

I quite get this, and is where on a personal level I am my own survivor of mental health, and why I write this book.

To share the story, and end stigma around the words mental and health.

So lets continue whilst I tell you this story of miss understanding, peril, fear, love and life.

With the purpose fulfilled with love to end the stigma around mental health and allow us to be conscious within our behaviours as humans towards each other.

I write this with love for my daughter Charis Mae who has kept me surviving, and is the beacon of light I shine upon.

# Introduction

I grew up in a small market town on the border of North and West Yorkshire, which is also well known for its Horse Racing.

Went through that life not quite knowing, or understanding why I felt something different.

Feeling pains around me in areas, headaches, stresses, and not knowing how or what that was that was affecting me.

Although I got on through life, listened to the 'imprints' around me, the 'stigma' lack of recognition and aptitude to the word mental as if it there is something seriously wrong with you.

Based upon aptitudes and thoughts from the 1900's pre and being passed on through society into 1970's-80's Britain around my younger years.

So to say or even believe or think that someone could have a part of there health that was mental, and not to work on that was why scarcity hit my brain in fear of recognition.

Mental Health is real, everyone suffers with mental health issues, some manifest this in other health issues through longer term ill health.

# Chapter 1

## Everything is Energy

Everything is Energy - $E = MC^2$ - Einstein

Do you realise that everything that you touch has its own sound wave, it's own energy, and as humans we also resonate on sound waves, frequencies, colour and the energy that is connected to the energy within everything that has been created.

This Energy is Universal

In essence this is the energy that we feel, naturally we hold a boundary around us to prevent people to our space.

And within a thought or a word the word 'mental', became related to the energy off something crazy, a person that could cause harm, someone that wasn't fit in the head, and other aspects or thought patterns and various reactions created around this word over the many years.

To be 'mental' in the mid 80's was to be cast away, locked in a home, cell, or a ward and kept numb by ill fitting drugs, and in a case in today's modern medicine still is to this within some degree by creating drugs to break the body, and drugs to cure the body.

To the same effect prescription and drugs in all forms which includes alcohol, caffeine, prescription, street drugs, veterinary drugs and many more within this list are all to be classed as a drug.

And yet what is a drug of the mind?

# Everything is Energy

Is the mind altered by 'drugs'? Or more than this!

What influenced you at school to make thought forms or opinions of others around mental health, or the way you may react to something?

What is a drug caused by the mind?

So where is the line between psychosis and genius if this is to be the answer?

There are many different views cast upon our societies around the world.

Religious aspects, class and society aspects, work aspects, peer aspects and many more.

All of these aspects have the ability to create for you to believe and take example of what they do, or to follow your own thoughts around what others may think.

Or think about you.

What if you wake up, and the 1st thing you say to yourself is.

*'Oh what a shit day, I cant believe its raining, dark, I've a hangover, my partner doesn't want me etc etc etc...'*

What sort of day are you creating for yourself if you are to think in this way?

Only that of a shit day !

And to behave and re-'act' in the way to how you are thinking about it.


So let's rephrase this.

What if you wake up, and the 1st thing you say to yourself is.

*'Oh My George, what a great day, I don't have to wash the windows or water my plants. OK I've got to get in the car or train/bus to work yet the air will be refreshed with the water, and its fun to be a child and jump in the puddles from time to time.'*

# Everything is Energy

Or if you don't have to go anywhere it gives you time to sit at home and write or read, or catch up on phoning friends.

What if you create your day or life within your thought process?

How can we 'reframe' our thoughts to be one of conscious thought so we create an amazing day everyday?

So to say is there a fine line between insanity and genius.

I say its simple, yes.

Anyone can over do anything, that only creates a form of stress, a case where if you had a bucket of balls, and you imagine each ball as a thought about whatever.

You come to a point sometimes where there isn't enough space within this bucket to full fill all the thoughts.

At this point you are at risk of not managing your mental health as well as possible, and your emotions may change, you feel ill, tired and more, The little things annoy you.

And yet do we every really look at our own mental health and say hi to it?

Check in on it and make sure it's OK?

Relate to the balls in the bucket and ask each aspect if its OK?

Do's it need support?

Is there to many balls in the bucket to cope with the thought that you most need to focus on?

Yourself !

Do we as humans act in a conscious way at times to recognize when people may have to many balls in that bucket, to take time to care, love and understand each other, or are we to busy thinking about our own self greed that we are creating a world where we don't care?

Take a moment to think about this one.

# Everything is Energy

Some people are more connected at feeling the energy I was talking about earlier. And is where the lack of understanding around the links between mental and physical health within the world community is at a miss.

What would it take to change the way that you think about how you react towards people that has compassion, about how you may feel from one day to the next and to react in a way towards everyone you meet with that same compassion, love and understanding?

To be one of consciousness, not of hate or fear, greed, miss understanding.

What does it take to make a difference within this world.

Only the way we think, and approach life, and the way we approach each other.

Everything is energy.

When we approach life with love, and creativity we bring that upon ourselves and share that with the people around us, and only create that sharing and love when we are creating a thought flow and reaction of love to engage in that energy.

So Lets begin

# Chapter 2

## Making sure things don't get on TOP

TOP– Trauma of Pain (Panic in the moment).

I love my amazing conscious friend Surina for helping me recognize this when things get on TOP of me, or maybe yourself.

I was supporting her to look after a property with so many different issues to resolve, tenants to deal with, maintenance etc when I came upon my own panic in the moment.

Which I love Surina at that moment in time for recognising within me, and being so loving and supportive to bring me to a level and state of mind in this moment to bring me to a stage where I was calm in the Panic of the moment.

It is also what prompted the name of the book.

How many things get on top of you on a day to day basis?

How many things do you then take that trauma of pain/panic in the moment and transfer that stress onto someone else and then make it there stress also, or blame it on another issue?

How many times do you allow things to get on TOP of you, and then transfer that onto another person around you.

Thus transferring that energy onto the next person around you.

# Making sure things don't get on TOP

What can we do to help each other when we sense a trauma of pain or panic in the moment with each other?

Do you get a headache or a pain when to many things get on top of you?

Or can you allow those things that get on top of you to be a pleasure and a joy within life, and not to allow that energy to drain you, for you to be frustrated, annoyed, irate and transfer that to someone else in maybe the way you speak with them, or relate your stress of things getting on top of you to only creates a state of panic of stress around us and the people we share that time with.

I admit I am not my own angel always when too many pressures and things get on TOP of me, yet I do recognise when this may happen now, and at least can take some form of control to apologise for the way I reacted because of the stress in the moment to control the moment from being out of control or an emotional consequence or drama.

Which is what too many people create in there lifestyles is only a thought to create a drama and not peace of mind with each other.

And yet how do we react to each other when these things are happening?

Example right now, I'm currently focusing on writing, and yet my cat Sox is persistently meowing at me directly under the keyboard whilst I'm trying to write, my friends dog toby running around my feet pursuing sox and following him everywhere and the same time my elderly dog standing in front of me.

I feel her eyes in my head as a headache.

Do I ?

Shout at sox, be frustrated at Tess for being stood under my feet, and take my energy of what is on top of me to be a frustration, which then I feel horrible about also, or do I switch off, and send my highest love to sox with light and allow myself to focus on writing and go with the flow.

How do you approach your children when they are around your feet, frustrating you, and taking your attention away from the focus on what your trying to do whilst your putting the shopping away, or maybe having a conversation about an important issue with a friend or colleague or your partner?

# Making sure things don't get on TOP

How do you react under pressure at work when exhausted, and react to your colleagues around you?

The reason I'm asking you these questions, is to ask you to check in on your own consciousness.

What do I mean by this?

Are you conscious about the way that you react around people, and the reaction you get back from them?

Do you react with a punch or with peace and love, and what reaction do you get back from how you react?

There are many frightened people within communities and frightening thoughts going on around us in the news, in the papers, and more. Yet what reaction are we getting back if we are only to react with a consciousness to be angry and frustrated at that.

Only one that is to be frightened, angry and frustrated at the world and people we share our time with and our circumstances with.

What if we are to change our consciousness as humans, and not sheep and think our own thoughts not polluted by fear, then think of the life we will create around us that will bring us harmony within each other, our works, our environments?

As another friend of mine Bevell says.

'Let that be your food for thought.'

How do you dissolve conflict within you and your life's?

Your relationships?

What consciousness or TOP do you put within your life to create a drama or trauma?

**Making sure things don't get on TOP**

What changes could you make to the way in how you react to someone and how you get a reaction back?

Even when someone is having a 'bad' day and sharing anger it is only because of the lack of love that the person has received from this.

Sometimes all they need to hear is

**'Its OK I love you, everything will be OK'.**

## Chapter 3

**Have we forgot how we react as humans too create a conscious society ?**

I feel that this is a good question we need to ask ourselves as human being

and wish to keep the next couple of chapters simple to thinking about the following thoughts and questions I want you to ask yourself.

What do we do with our day to day life's?

Do you have a community around you that is supportive and speaks with each other?

What is it that inspires us, full fills our time, our days

What in essence is our purpose in day to day life?

Have you checked in on your own mental health today and said hi to it?

# Chapter 4

## Air to clear and dissolve it

Its sunny outside and its funny I should come to talk about this, because I came to a short block in flow of thought and writing and used the above example to clear using

Air too heal the mind and space to allow the thoughts to flow.

What you create in your thoughts are the actions you take.

Our limitations come from our brain, and in the programming we have had drummed into us since our earliest years.

This system carries an inertia within us, because we continue to re produce this and introduce generation on generation off children into the limited systems we believe in.

Or as Sidra Jafri would say when you come to a block within yourself its then when its the time to keep going staying positive and moving forward and connecting the most.

What do you do to stop the blocks?

**Chapter 5**

**Social Media Sites and lack of 'connection'**

We are avatars within a society stuck behind spending more time on mobile phones or social media connecting with each other.

Rather than spending our time in real communication with each other.

The human touch has been so lost in modern day society, and connection is forcing the world towards being on our phones or laptops to connect and integrate with each other.

In essence we are only avatars floating around in cyber space wanting to connect, yet missing the touch or aspect of true connection.

For example only yesterday was I taking a short rail journey seeing 4 friends sat opposite each other, not speaking or talking or communicating, just glued to each others phones.

Or the rest of the world as bubbles with headsets on or focused on our own self without paying attention to companionship and contact.

An aspect of this has been shown on Black Mirror on Netflix showing how in a future world we as avatars are rated on our interaction through our future version of mobile tech.

Which rates us on who we can interact with or to what value of service we will receive by who rates us on our day to day interaction with each other.

The lower the points you are given the lower the aspects of society you are allowed to engage with ..

# Social Media Sites and lack of 'connection'

Is the world coming to us only judging each other through our phones, or is it coming to a phase were connectiveness is at our roots, and our avatars are only an addition of pressure to us to connect with this world.

I myself need to write content and connect through social media in this modern world through blogs Facebook twitter etc and yet have learnt that the only content I wish to promote is of positive content or value.

How do you promote yourself to be on social media?

What words do you portray?

Are they to pick fault or create good from what you see?

So many Facebook groups for example are spent on the time criticising others rather than taking positive action and creating a positive outcomes and circumstances that we are lost in translation of what is right or wrong with each other.

How does this impact our mental health as a society. ?

Some research was done on some dating sites to see what sort of reaction people will give you.

In essence in some state if people are there only for a positive relationship or to connect then why if someone states they wish to connect is that perceived in 85+% of responses to a degree of pre judgement that a person is only wanting sex.

So in what way does this in a reality make our avatars work and think.

And what judgements and thoughts and reactions are we creating for each other when we are only responding in a way to create a viewpoint of someone or perception that a person is only seeking this or that, when be real this is only your viewpoint and judgement and reaction to the words or things you hear or see.

So what sort of reaction do you expect to receive when your thoughts or judgements you are making are creating the reaction of your own.

Your responsible for what you attract to yourself, or repel by the thoughts your creating and the words you use to interact.!

**Chapter 6**


**Our Monkey Minds**


Do you ever cross conflict yourself in the way you re act or re en act to something.

Just this morning I put my TOP onto another friend in a message saying I'm in 2 minds what to do today, because at the weekend I have 2 important study sessions, and mi back from a few days what was to be a break yet with little sleep and I have a load to catch up on at home pay the rent and had promised to help support my friend get his garden ready.

Thus in essence in a bit of a Tis Woz with myself not knowing or thinking if to let my friend down or to work on me to allow time to do that another time.

The problem with gardens is working around the weather in time also, and today is a suitable day for that not to warm, dry, and around 20C comfortable with a little moisture in the air allowing the ground to be turned easier.

Yet the universe has my back.
My friend simply responded to me Stop with your Monkey Mind.

In other words – stop overthinking, have no judgement Just allow the universe to have your back and do what you do.

# Our Monkey Minds

2 mins later I receive a text from my friend understanding. And saying OK lets do this on Monday instead.

Although this is overlapping things, I allow the universe to have my back and time to be when times should be right to do things and work on the things that they needed.

So I say thank you to Yvette for bringing me to write a chapter about your Monkey Mind, how it over thinks things at times and puts pressure on you and maybe others indirectly... More to write about this soon

**Chapter 7**

## When there's too much on TOP

### TOP – Transference of Pressure / Trauma of Pain

So here comes the key aspect of why mi writing this book.

The recognition of Transference of pressure.

How this can make you ill, mentally affect you, create an imbalance to you as a human being.

I've recently had a lot going on, I've written an aspect of this within my blog also.

It made me ill, tired worn out, unable to function,

So I had to STOP!

Literally stop everything I was doing to support other people and work on myself to get better from this. 10 yr s in recovery is the real aspect and more, yet recently I was at a point where I felt I was breaking back to where I was 10 yr s ago, because the transference of all the pressure (TOP) that was going on around me made me physically unwell, and that affected my mental and emotional behaviour also.

# When there's too much on TOP

Fortunately spirit had my back and was holding onto my spiritual connection this time in recognition of where I had fell apart last time, and this time I made sure I STOPPED to regain mind, energy, spirit and physical issues, although a trapped nerve down my right side is causing me shooting pains whilst writing this is maybe what my own guides tell me as the pain or lessons of the past reminding you and this clearing ?

Admittedly some could believe this, yet they say that the body holds memories of events and this is caused as pain.

Thus 33yrs of trauma prior to my mental breakthrough 10 yr s ago.

So what have been the pressures I recognised recently. ?

- Threat of financial losses causing a risk of homelessness again
- A relationship breakthrough and a friend moving away
- your daughters mum calling you a crank etc and still being negatively abusive making excuses to not allow you to have contact with your daughter and behaving in a narcissistic way.
- My elderly dog needing as much attention as a baby child 24/7
- My body becoming run down and illness caused by stress of the above which literally crippled me from doing anything for anyone else let alone barely look after self for 3-4 weeks, debilitating condition of longer term mental pressures causing an illness to self

This is where the systems in place at this current moment in the UK and most of the whole world are debilitating people.

Why? Because they aren't based around empowering people?

They are based around greed, pressure, stress and to bring people to there knees if they're not in a place of abundance.

So what can we do to make sure we don't apply to much on TOP to people?

Is this within our own consciousness when we are interacting ?

# When there's too much on TOP

The famous Author Sidra Jafri of the book Awakening states a simple factor relating to how we create our own abundance in life.

Its simply way of saying 'What you are focusing on becomes abundant'

So if say we are focusing on a fault about something then we are often to pick fault about this, and this is what we create.

How can we use this same principle to ensure that we work on working with people with compassion and recognition, and when things get on top we have recognition of this, and don't transfer it as a pressure to someone else.

You can easily place a thought about your children,

E.g. a friend asks you how your child is.

You say to your friend that they are

'Grumpy, and always mischievous'

,so this creates an imprint within your child and your friend that this is there behaviour, or even a transference of pressure to create that child to behave in a grumpy of mischievous way.

So next time your relate to your children be careful of how you relate to them to other people.

More about that later this relates to having a principle of

'No Judgement',

you can read more about this in 'The Awakening' by Sidra Jafri.

All of us make a judgement to some extent.

# When there's too much on TOP

It is often that we relate to this judgement in a way that may create a pressure or a transference of our own judgement, in a way of reaction that may cause a negative or positive response upon the way you may have reacted by your own judgement Thus if you have no judgement you react with your own consciousness and not the judgement of others around you.

Or reacting to peer pressure to respond in a way which maybe inappropriate

When we have no judgement we only react with love and compassion.

Back to TOP – Remember that your Transference of pressure is often only a transference of your own pain onto someone else.

I admit recently I have been experiencing my own TOP, and where I have placed that onto others that worked in good ways or bad ways. It depends on how you see life.

Everything is but a learning, not a mistake or a fault, simply learnings.

It's what you make of these learnings is how you progress your life.

You either keep living from the same learning and repeating the same error, or you move on and recognise that a learning is just a learning.

And its just the universe's way of teaching you to accept life as it is, and be grateful for every moment in it, or maybe to learn to be more compassionate.

Because when you focus your energy or thought on a fault then it becomes just a pain in the arse for someone else to deal with.

Or your own transference of that fault creating more faults and then your living and spending your time in nothing but a fault based life.

Remember everything is energy, this even comes down to the energy or thoughts you create and the reactions that those thoughts create.

# Chapter 8

## Creating 'Sukhmani' = 'peace of mind'

If your looking for failure in everything you will only find that failure within it.

So be mindful of how you make judgement about things and to what reaction this could lead you to make.

Some people are amazing at the way they approach people with listening compassion and ensuring that the words they use are responsible to prompt a calm responsible reaction from life and how people may react to them.

Others are completely mindless, unaware and react in a way to blame others and only make life and times and there own focus with regards to relation to blaming others.

The question we need to ask ourselves is.

How can we create a peace within our own mind

if maybe we are only seeking an outcome of failure out of a situation?

Think back quickly to how we wake up and create our thoughts.

Our judgement and thought process and conscript is to be analytical or computer like to only create outcomes within our life's, our work, or even our relationships with others as an outcome of failure.

What do we do to make a judgement within what someone may say to us to react in a way where our judgement with our words may serve an outcome of the opposite ?

# Creating 'Sukhmani' = 'peace of mind'

Do you go around bullying people, making them to blame for everything being wrong in your life (Narcissism), and then blame people for something they have said or done as an excuse for you to create there life to be a hell or a misery, and only portray upon people that they are to blame for there words or behaviour, when maybe it is only a reaction to the energy you have portrayed to them in the first instance.

I've personally been a victim of this in my past life before my breakdown or should I say breakthrough, which taught my own learnings from going through this were to help me recognise my own empath skills or what is classed as anxiety, or displacement of energy as I like to call it.

When you learn to recognise these skills that you have that are only labelled as mental health issues in society, then you become the master of controlling your own peace of mind through the awareness and consciousness of your own energy, or the displacement of the energy around you, that being around these type of people or lack of love and compassion affects your emotions.

Which is also a lack of understanding of mental health and the reactions you may receive from society around you, your pears, your family, your colleagues.

And is often when they are simply unconscious to the energy and reactions they are making around you because of the astigmatism caused by society

When you become in tuned within this energy then you are able to shield yourself from the negative emotions of society and people who are not yet awakened

in reality your responsible for the shit you create by your own positive or negative or destructive narcissistic viewpoint

What do kids do when they are name calling in a playground, and how does the emotional reaction of a name call often lead to an explosive fight from nothing.

If we as adults are to resolve life by only looking for a fault and creating one then we are only behaving like these children in that playground resolving life like children, and not as adults.

# Creating 'Sukhmani' = 'peace of mind'

And this is where being responsible for what you dish out in words reaction and life can serve you the correct or incorrect reaction or action or in reality the outcome you really want from life.

Yet we have a major issue outlining these factors, such as what the newspapers say to us, what our phone advertises us, what the media says about war, games made to this effect, crime, and a system created around us to only make us react to life in fear and to be unconscious about it.

It's when we come out of the recognition that we are only beings being lead to believe and react to people that way because of what we have been told or lead to believe, or even about ancestral history or wars or even the bible, Koran or other scriptures which say to us that life should be this way.

Is only when we react to humanity in life to respect it in the way to create a peace of mind with everything and everybody around us.

Because at the end of the day, if you want to choose a life of misery.

You create it within your own matrix of reality or the thoughts you create about others, so you only react and live a life of being that way to others, and keep repeating this behaviour.

Between the ages of 0-7 your own type of behaviour is imprinted into you by whatever circumstances or imprints from the world are around you at moment in time that was being created

The human physiology continues to behave and copy repeat this behaviour every 7 years as you either go through life or grow through life.

0-7 imprint
7-14 copy repeat imprints develop others around these imprints
14-21 copy repeat
21-28 copy repeat
28-35 etc

So in a sense I hope this relationship to how we react to life and copy the behaviours around us are only the conscripts of the matrix within our mind that we have developed as a way we believe we should behave to one another.

# Creating 'Sukhmani' = 'peace of mind'

When you work this bit out, and recognise behaviours or patterns within your own behaviour or outcomes that either create stress or trauma, or the opposite a mindfulness of peace, then you are at peace of mind within yourself.

And this is where we are at peace of mind.

Yet as a society are we reacting to create a peace of mind or environment for each other or are we so self centred that we simply couldn't care less for each other?

Admittedly life throws us challenges to test our harmony of our own minds and souls.

I've been at the other end of the spectrum 10 year ago myself when In essence life threw its challenges at me, and because of the overflow of information my brain was unable to handle so much stress and trauma and came to a point of shut down.

It took me until around 7 or 8 years ago to recognise I had actually gone through that, and yet was not aware of the fact that the mind creates its own conscripts, yet the learnings of living through the darkness were only teaching to never allow itself to go back to that point.

Although the systems and beliefs of the way we are as a human society aren't designed to help us achieve this!

The system is designed to break us not empower us unless we are within the higher realm of light ourselves or the recognition of this and to be conscious to create a future where there is a peace of mind.

If not what is the world to coming to when we are closely approaching the year 2020 ?

**Chapter 9**

## Are computers just like people?

Yes

If there's too much going on inside its memory, it simply shuts itself down and stops working.....

We as humans are exactly the same..

Our brain is one massive super computer

On a morning how do we wake ourselves up?

A tea, a coffee, a shower.

Sometimes we wake up were our energy is blocked, our brain is coming to its senses, and computers are exactly the same.

Yet they only have a small capacity of the computing power of the brain which is a massive super computer.

Computers always seem to have a glitch or a bug within them.

If our computer breaks down, we make sure we take the time to fix that glitch so that we get it working.

Do we always do the same with our own brain?

# Are computers just like people?

Do we de-clutter those glitches that keep us from stopping moving forward.

And how can we do this?

Here's a great example of myself at this moment in time writing this in the divine spirit of the universe.

I had woken this morning, quite exhausted after travelling the last week taking a mental break in amazing Croatia.

Set early alarms to continue with my study program with the school of awakening. To be spending my first 20-30 mins or so attempting to access the programme because there were some technical glitches with the computing systems.

In a state of slightly UN awakeness this causes a pressure or transference of trauma onto other members of the team to get this issue working from myself.

Maybe a slight reasoning for frustration because the systems weren't working and whatever else came up at that time because both my own computer at that time, my brains computer at that time, and the teams plug ins aren't functioning as they should....

Lets rephrase this.

There was a reason for this, it prompted me to write this chapter in the moment relating to the way we relay our thoughts and often have blocks and glitches within our own computers.

To be awakened around this, a team member recognised my own computer had shut down a little and to take an energy shower to resolve this.

What do I mean by this?

I was at a point of not being awake, in every sense. This causing my emotions to react in frustration and a little stress at the time.

# Are computers just like people?

Clearing the energy within this facet with the energy shower, created a recognition within myself I was reacting in a state of transference of pressure, one from being frustrated the systems weren't working to a state of recognition that energy is everything, there are reasons for SHIT happening

Something Happened In Time – SHIT "Sidra Jafri"

I was to come to awaken my senses to accept that the systems weren't working on the study portal, that's no issue because in this moment it has helped me to focus on scripting another chapter in flow in around 20 mins, and to love the divine and the universe for prompting me to re program the original way my own brain was working at that moment in time.

Lets make some sense of what I've written on the previous page and

take a quick thought on this for a moment.

See where you get frustrated at things, and instead of carrying on this way becoming stressed and making your energy to be low.

Cover your body with a shower of sparkling light, refresh your mind.

And work on where in that moment you can create a little magic and something positive and release trauma or your transference of that pain of pressure onto something or someone else.

Which only brings us back to When there's to MUCH on TOP... Just STOP

# Chapter 10

## Too much on TOP

My own life has been within many pressure points recently, and at many a time have I transferred my own pressure on others to help support to many balls in my own bucket.

My own parents I have been trying to make an understanding of what is support, what can be empowering, what wasn't empowering, and how to move forward through this with regards to the lack of awareness and understanding, or even maybe a systematic belief system that we are surrounded by that makes us take our own pressures out on other people with out a thought to how we are applying these pressures.

Or to even how they can affect each other if our communication in thought or reaction to a person who maybe is in need of support, someone to explain there situation to, someone to reach out to in despair when there's to many pressures going on around them to enable them to cope in that moment in life,

What we can do as people, so that when there is to much on top with people, or a trigger of a past event which may cause fear of this repeating itself again.

Is to recognise how and where we transfer our traumas of our pains, or our trauma of experience around each other, to what results we achieve in the way that we respond to this.

# Too much on TOP

Do we respond to people when we see them in trauma with ignorance which may cause more trauma because then the person who is reaching out within there soul to connect to each other in compassion is not receiving the love or support we are in need of.

Because we are judging our thought towards a person without love understanding.

Which indirectly causes more trauma and fear within each other.

Because we are not creating an environment between each other of compassion love or thought.

Let me try and explain this with regards to mental health and anxiety.

Most people when they are in trauma or panic or expressing where they need help are in a state of panic or trauma...

The first thing that anyone needs to do is to create an atmosphere around them which is to calm them in that situation.

Most peoples programmings are to react and to say something like get a grip of yourself, or if you end up behaving this way it will create this for you,

Or mi not taking your mood today and mi ignoring you. Your fit for a loony bin. Go and see a doctor...

What sort of reaction or outcome do you think that this sort of sound we are creating will create for the person in trauma ?

The first thing we need to do is listen.

What are we doing within this world to create time for this?

# Too much on TOP

Are we creating a judgement within our thoughts which allows us to excuse ourselves for this?

To make the other person to blame within our thoughts to react in a way of non communication and lack off support?

Or to react with love and the awareness to assess the needs of those around us we love to give them the support they need.

If they need a roof over there heads.

And you have the abundance to help them, there your friend you know them, you trust them, give them your love give them that roof so then that person has stability.

Create an environment around them where they can be calm and what you are saying and how you are reacting to them is inspiring and will help empower them.

Understand that everyone is equal.

We all have mental health issues. And at any moment in time can our mental health affect us.

When there's to Much on Top this becomes a breakdown.

When we can recognise and support this we prevent this and create breakthroughs for each other

Some peoples minds and bodies are at so much imbalance or confusion of the lifestyles or lack of understanding or compassion or love that they become misaligned within themselves, imbalanced.

If we are to create an environment for people or a life of imbalance then what are we creating for them.?


So when there's too much on TOP next time.

Stop and think for a minute about how your reacting to this person is supporting them or your creating it an issue for you and being unconscious to be love..

# Too much on TOP

How if you are at the other side of this can you then be a person who is empowering towards them.

Compassionate and too create a space for each other.

Where our mental healths are not in anguish.

We as humans have evolved into a state of who we truly are which is one of love and compassion and consciousness.

**Chapter 11**

## The fine line between mental health

What if we are just travellers being sent messages from our ancestral past or for the future through a stream of consciousness and light ?

Nikola Tesla theorised this and at the time was cast astray as mental or disillusioned and it is only now that we are recognizing that his theory was correct, and that we are all quantum energy particles and only beings made up of atoms of tiny light.

Truth has been exposed around the manipulation of sound frequencies within music retuning to 440Mhz which prior to 1939 was 432Mhz.

Why was this done?

432Mhz is the frequency of harmony and balance.

Play this sound against water and see the differences between 440Mhz, and 432.. just think our bodies are 80% water.

What can this do to the body within?

This also affects our consciousness or flow of cl-air senses.

# The fine line between mental health

As humans we all are to some effect each have these abilities

Clair Voyance - Sight

Clair Audience - Hearing

Clair Sentience - Feeling

Clair Congicence – Knowing

Clair Factory - Smell

Maybe mental health is because our clair senses are at an imbalance because the frequency of sound was changed universally ? Make your own viewpoint about this, yet check out you-tube on sound frequencies and Tesla.

It was recognised by a Russian Scientist mid 1930's that the body and mind or frequencies we naturally resonate on to be disorganised thus creating a sound of illness.

Maybe cancer and illnesses are a cause where the body is unable to heal as naturally as possible because the sound waves it is receiving aren't in harmony. I'm sure anyone who is reading this book who is pre war had a sense of happiness and more peace within them prior to the disruptions in sound.

Sound-waves are generated by light and frequency.

For further research in this I admit, I am no master quantum physicist yet this is where the basics of the universe align, and to what effect with the world population being at a mass where we have now come to a stage where food supply is not enough to cover the population and this is a sign of the system seeking its way to reduce that?

# The fine line between mental health

So what is mental health ?

In reality it is only a flow of misalignment of our thoughts, in a universe which is causing a confusion about it and manipulating our thoughts with numb ill fitting drugs, rather than supplying it with light love, colour and consciousness.

What if as Nikola Tesla said that his ideas came to him in his consciousness from a source of light.

Therefore aren't we all messengers to each other to wake up to check in on our mental health more, after all we check in on our physical health.

What's the excuse ?

Isn't our mental health maybe just a misalignment of what our unconscious mind is telling us when our bodies maybe misaligned.

Do you not suffer with stress when you are physically more run down, or suffer with physical illness when your mind is not working to its best.

Are you talking to your body through your mind based on teaching your body through your mind that you heal it.

As it is your own belief that you create about your own illness, and to that end where that belief of how your illness is affecting you based upon the thoughts of what we are generating about it.

Sometimes the pains are just reminders to the mind that we are not working on that area of our body, or are trapped memories from a past event that we hold onto that pain and keep holding within us, which causes the trauma or tumour within our body.

Therefore are we just travellers of time within our own memory and mind creating a mindset within our own consciousness which is creating the outcomes we create from our life?

Lets rephrase the world educating around our minds, our body's, our beliefs, because we classify this as our mental health, our physical health, our spiritual health (belief), which all comes to the affect of our Emotional Health.

# The fine line between mental health

Within ourselves we create our own outcomes, and the belief systems we are creating around mental health.

Isn't it time that we start focusing on all aspects of our health ?

So then we are at a balance, and not a confusion of what our consciousness is, in the belief off which is were we as human souls are creating a consciousness of mental health, or physical health, or our church or religious belief which is what creates our emotional thoughts about our life's around us.

When we are in a system of judgement where we are not to focus on creating a harmony within ourselves to balance these beliefs.

Then how can we be classed as being mental?

**Chapter 12**

## Insanity Genius Or Consciousness ?

The Fine Line between genius insanity and consciousness.

What is our consciousness?

This is what we create from our thoughts.

It is the energy that surrounds us in light, in nature, in what we created as human beings for our lifestyles.

It is as one where we are all connected through our memory, our implants, our cross genesised DNA over the generations, and our belief systems about our society.

Personally my research into my own life came from wanting to understand what I had personally been through, and where after 10 years the writing comes into consciousness, insanity as maybe defined by those who don't understand it, or the universal energy of light that we are all connected to.

Have you ever been thinking about calling someone, and suddenly they message or call you, this is known as what our clair cognicence or knowing is about, our thoughts projecting to one another because we are consciously al connected from light which forms our DNA

# Insanity Genius Or Consciousness ?

Recognize yourself s in the glitches happening around you

" What sounds are you creating about other people when no one can hear your thoughts ?

The things that we say we want we don't actually want, what we want is a feeling... "

(Conscious Upgrade Chat- Sidra Jafri)

## #Oh_My_George

Lets rephrase the word mental health to mental wealth

Then we are creating a sound and consciousness of mental wellness in our health only one of being mentally well and encouraging that sound creates a cure or an acceptance that we all have an element of our conscious wellness within our mental and clair senses..

Maybe then we can create an equilibrium of our healths, and maybe the sound that we resonate within our thoughts about our healths is complete in structure.

One that is consciously connected to each other.

The recognition that all health issues are surrounded by the sound we create within our consciousness about them.

And maybe, just maybe

we can create a sound within the world were we each have a mindset that we have equal (SPEM)

Spiritual Wholeness

Physical Wellness

Emotional Balance

Mental Wealth

# Insanity Genius Or Consciousness ?

A computer filters its SPAM so lets rephrase our own mindsets each day, to not only be connected to each other, so that we create the sounds of love compassion support.

The we start creating connection within community again.

When we check in on our own SPEM on a daily basis.

Check in to see if our own consciousness or our complete body is in check and in harmony.

The resonance of sound-waves can create an imbalance around us within our own energy fields which can disturb our consciousness.

So we always need to ensure that to create a mentally well society we cut out the filters of negative pollution from our environment and start to reconnect as human beings, make days where our mobiles are not connected.

Go back to the old times of sitting as families and friends sharing meals not isolating yourself in your box which the system has created for us to be like.

And become a world of conscious people who think in a conscious way, who excel in our humanity.

Learn to connect with the other 80-90 ish DNA strands that we haven't yet been taught fully how to utilise.

Then we become the source of light that we are all inter connected by because it is all around us which gives us the energy sources that we create around us.

Take the matrix for example!

To be conscious of this, to be mindful of who we are, to be compassionate and resonate sounds within ourselves and outside of us, that only create a conscious society can we create that within us, as our inner souls are taught to.

# Insanity Genius Or Consciousness ?.

Maybe mental health is just a misalignment of the true clair abilities that we have as human beings. It is certainly a misalignment of the viewpoints and thoughts cast about it!

And maybe just maybe society has been hiding that from us....???

Maybe just maybe we will all soon see as the more of us who wake up to the world of a system which is telling us to numb down our clair senses, with ill fitting prescription drugs and we see more and more children and a world suffering with anxiety traumas seeing things, hearing voices, and maybe even other inter dimensional beings, who knows what the future will bring us.

Maybe the unconscious around us will wake up?

Be also conscious that the worlds population is at a demand where our food or water resources are being wasted how longer can we as a world continue to cope with this.

We will see for ourselves when we are truly awakened beings working together within our collected consciousness as the ancient Mesopotamian scriptures suggest that maybe we will start seeing the truths unfold.

Yet that's another story.

For now

I say thank you And be conscious these are only my viewpoints.

The main message here is to be conscious about how we react to each other.

To be conscious about our thoughts and what they create around us and for us.

To be conscious to create a mentally wealthy outcome for everyone..

Thank you to the universe for inspiring me to create this with passion to make a difference to mental health world wide.

Have an amazing day wherever you are in the world right now.

# Insanity Genius Or Consciousness ?

It is my wish for this book to be shared so we wake up to the way we are reacting to mental health and create a world of mental wealth.

I have designed this book to be read in under an hour to pass onto a friend, or even leave on a bus or train or airplane and to give them an insight into what being conscious about our thoughts is, and the way that we approach everything in life,

How this can make such a huge difference to the way we approach and live our life's and the people we interact with.

Most of all our impact upon our mental healths.

Have an amazing day.

Sending tons of colours of love and light to everyone who will read this within the universe.

George

1st Published 1st December 2018

**Further Readings**

Sidra Jafri – The Awakening – 9 Principles to change your life – Watkins 2015

Andy Harrington – Passion Into Profit, 2015, reprint 2017

Daniel Goldman – Working with Emotional Intelligence

Imanuel Valikovsy – Mankind In Amnesia

wwe.schoolofawakening.com/cuc (every Sunday live)

Posted   2   3   2 /9 .
           20/12/2018      - LOCATION LS28 8AL.

                            with love.

                            thankyou to

                            everyone.

                            George.

Thankyou Amazon
          PL for party.

Printed in Poland
by Amazon Fulfillment
Poland Sp. z o.o., Wrocław